D1541612

THE EMPIRE BUILDERS

THE EMPIRE BUILDERS

BY BORIS VIAN

TRANSLATED FROM THE FRENCH BY SIMON WATSON TAYLOR

GROVE PRESS, INC., NEW YORK

Les Bâtisseurs d'Empire was first produced by the Théâtre Nationale Populaire, under the direction of Jean Vilar, at the Théâtre Recamier, Paris, on December 22, 1959. Costumes and décor by André Acquart, music by Georges Delerue, production by Jean Negroni, and with the following cast:

FATHER	Henri Virloguex
MOTHER	Madeleine Cheminat
ZENOBIA	Dany Saval
MUG	Armande Navarre
NEIGHBOR	Yves Péneau
THE SCHMÜRZ	Isaac Alvarez

The Empire Builders was first produced by the San Francisco Actors Workshop, under the direction of Marc Estrin, at the Encore Theater, San Francisco, February 19, 1966. Costumes by Nancy Bond, designs by Carl Worth, sound effects by Susan Darby and Bill Maginnis, and with the following cast:

FATHER	Michael Linenthal
MOTHER	Jane Steckle
ZENOBIA	Celeste Sarlatte
MUG	Marsha Efron
NEIGHBOR	Bert Brauer
THE SCHMÜRZ	Robert Skundberg

ACT ONE

The action takes place in a room with no special character, furnished in a conventional bourgeois manner, with a horrible antique sideboard along the back wall and a dining table and chairs all in one corner; windows with closed shutters; doors leading wherever necessary; and in the corner opposite the table the top of a staircase apparently leading up from a room which one presumes to be underneath, linking up with a staircase apparently leading to a room which would be on the floor above.

The stage is empty of people, even when the curtain is down, and remains empty when the curtain rises. From the staircase, approaching voices can now be heard from below.

FATHER'S VOICE (*urgently*): Come on, Anna, hurry up . . . only five more steps.

A sound of stumbling can be heard, then a cry.

I've told you already not to put your hand just where I put my feet, Zenobia . . . you've no sense of discipline, that's *your* trouble.

ZENOBIA'S VOICE (*trembling*): And why do you always have to be the first one up, eh?

FATHER'S VOICE (*terrified*): Shut up . . .

One can hear, coming from outside, a noise that is

*frightening to hear but difficult to describe. A deep
reverberating noise with overtones of shrill throbbing.*

ZENOBIA's VOICE (*calm*): I'm scared . . .

FATHER's VOICE: Quick . . . one last effort! . . .

*He appears in the room, carrying a toolbox and some
planks. He falls down, picks himself up and looks
around him. Meanwhile, the rest of his family emerges:*
ZENOBIA, *the daughter, is sixteen or seventeen years
old.* ANNA, *the mother, is thirty-nine or forty. The*
FATHER *himself is over fifty, and bearded. Finally there
is the maid, whose name is* MUG.

*Everyone is weighed down with parcels and suitcases.
Already, in one corner, the schmürz is waiting. It is
completely wrapped up in bandages, and dressed in
rags. One of its arms is in a sling. It is holding a walking stick in its free hand. It limps, bleeds, and is ugly
to look at. It cowers in its corner.*

FATHER: We're nearly there, children. Come on, jump to it.

*The Noise can be heard once more in the street, that
is to say outside the windows.* ZENOBIA *snivels.*

MOTHER: Now, now, my darling . . .

She goes toward ZENOBIA *to caress her, but the* FATHER
stops her.

FATHER: Anna! Give me a hand quickly. This is more
important.

*He rushes to the staircase and begins to bar the down-
ward flight of stairs with planks; she runs to help him
and, midway, sees the schmürz, stops suddenly, glares
at it and shrugs her shoulders.*

Hold the plank while I find a nail. *(He searches in his toolbox and finds a nail.)* I should really fix it with screws, but that would raise a whole set of problems.

MOTHER: Why?

FATHER: First of all, I haven't got any screws. Secondly, I haven't got a screwdriver. Thirdly, I never know which way to turn a screwdriver around.

MOTHER: This way . . . *(She shows him, the wrong direction.)*

FATHER: No, it's like this . . .

He shows her, the right direction. Meanwhile, the noise in the street grows louder. ZENOBIA *screams with rage.*

ZENOBIA: Well, hurry up, can't you!

FATHER: What am I thinking of . . . and you encouraging me to dawdle. *(He nails.)*

MOTHER: What do you mean, *me* encouraging you to dawdle?

FATHER: Let's not argue, my love. *(He throws himself upon her and kisses her violently.)* Ooh, you really give me ideas . . . *(He returns to his plank.)*

ZENOBIA: I'm hungry.

MOTHER: Mug, give the child something to eat.

During all this time, the maid has been busy arranging things, being careful to steer clear of the schmürz.

MUG: Yes, ma'am. *(To* ZENOBIA:*)* Do you want eggs, milk,

a cheese soufflé, porridge, chocolate, coffee, bread and butter, apricot jam, grapes, fruit, vegetables?

ZENOBIA: No, I want to eat.

MUG (*holding out a packet of biscuits to her*): All right, eat that, since you don't want anything.

She passes in front of the schmürz and shrinks away visibly. The FATHER *puts down his hammer and gets up.*

FATHER: Whew! . . . That's that . . . Now we can relax a bit. (*He stretches himself.*)

MOTHER: Leather should be cheap this year.

FATHER: What's that?

MOTHER: I said, leather should be cheap this year. The cows are stretching themselves. It's an old Norman proverb. You ought to know it.

FATHER: Why should I know it?

MOTHER: Don't you remember you used to be a horse knacker in Normandy? In the old days? Before all this?

FATHER: No . . . it had slipped my mind.

MOTHER: At Arromanches . . .

FATHER: Ah? Well, well. (*He scratches his beard.*) That's very strange. (*He goes up to the schmürz, slaps it as hard as he can, then returns, still pensive.*) What you've just said astounds me.

MOTHER: Why?

FATHER: It astounds me, that's all. I'd completely forgotten.

(*He claps his hands.*) Well, Mug, is everything ship-shape at last? (*He inspects the room.*) It's nice here.

The MOTHER *goes up to the schmürz and kicks it several times.*

ZENOBIA (*looking at the sideboard*): It's horrible.

FATHER: What? Don't you like it here?

ZENOBIA: How long is this going to go on? How many more times are we going to be forced to rush out like this in the middle of the night, leaving half our things behind, all the places we know, the sun, the trees . . .

FATHER: But listen, we're still doing fine . . . look at this staircase . . .

MOTHER: Oh, there's nothing so marvelous in that; the child's right as far as that's concerned.

FATHER: Come now, it's not so bad. One can climb a staircase like that even in complete darkness . . . (*He experiments by dashing smartly up the stairs, then comes down again.*)

MOTHER: It's not as good as the last one.

FATHER: I'd say it's just the same. (*He dusts his hands.*)

ZENOBIA: How can you tell such lies? Downstairs I had my own room.

FATHER: What do you mean? Downstairs, we had three rooms, just as we do here. You slept in the living room.

ZENOBIA: No, no, I'm not talking about yesterday . . . I mean, downstairs, long before . . .

FATHER (*to the* MOTHER): She had her own room?

MOTHER: I don't remember very well. (*To* ZENOBIA:) You had your own room?

ZENOBIA: Yes, I had my own room; next to yours, facing the little sitting room.

MOTHER: What little sitting room?

ZENOBIA: The little sitting room with the dark-red armchairs and the Venetian mirror and the pretty red silk curtains. The red carpet and the gilt chandelier.

MOTHER: Zenobia, are you sure you know what you're talking about?

ZENOBIA: Yes, I *do* know what I'm talking about.

FATHER: Well, I don't remember that. . . . Consequently, how could you, a mere child . . .

ZENOBIA: That's just why. It's the young who remember. Old people forget everything.

FATHER: Zenobia, show some respect for your parents.

ZENOBIA: There were six rooms.

MOTHER: Six rooms! Goodness! What a business to keep clean!

ZENOBIA: And Mug had her own room, too! And *that* wasn't there!

FATHER: What wasn't there?

ZENOBIA: *That!* (*She points at the motionless schmürz.*)

There is a very long silence.

MOTHER (*carefully*): Zenobia, my dear child, what are you talking about?

FATHER: Zenobia, you'd better lie down and rest.

Meanwhile MUG *has exited left. The* FATHER *and* MOTHER *approach* ZENOBIA.

MOTHER: You can see quite well there's nothing here. (*She goes up to the schmürz and attacks it viciously.*) You can see quite well. (*She is panting.*)

ZENOBIA (*unsurely*): We had six rooms . . . we were alone there . . . trees in front of the windows.

FATHER (*shrugs his shoulders*): Trees! (*He goes up to the schmürz and rains blows upon it.*) Trees. (*He rubs his hands together.*)

ZENOBIA: The bathroom was so pretty and white.

MUG *re-enters.*

MUG: Sir . . .

FATHER: What is it now?

MUG: There are only two rooms here, so where am I going to sleep?

FATHER: Well . . . We'll go into the other room, my wife, my daughter and myself . . . and you can sleep in here . . .

MUG (*decisively and coldly*): No!

FATHER (*laughs, annoyed*): No . . . she says no, just like that . . . well . . . hmm . . .

MOTHER (*to* FATHER): You could put up a partition. (*To* MUG, *severely:*) Well, will you be so good as to make up your mind?

MUG (*shrugs her shoulders*): If he puts up a partition . . .

(*She goes up to the schmürz and hits it dispiritedly.*) With a partition, I don't mind sleeping in here . . .

She shrugs her shoulders again, and goes back into the second room, taking some utensils with her. A silence.

ZENOBIA: You see . . . There are only two rooms. I knew.

The FATHER *has sat down; he has a rather disconcerted air, for the first time.*

FATHER: Two rooms . . . that's not so bad . . . there are people living in less space than that . . .

ZENOBIA (*frightened*): But even so, why . . . why . . .

MOTHER: Why what?

ZENOBIA: Why do we leave each time we hear the noise?

The FATHER *and* MOTHER *both look down.*

What is this noise? Tell me, tell me, mother . . .

MOTHER: Zenobia, my little angel, you've been told a hundred times not to ask that.

FATHER (*evasively*) : We don't know what it is ourselves. If we knew, we'd tell you.

ZENOBIA: But usually you know everything.

FATHER: Usually, yes. But that's just it, this is an exceptional circumstance. And then, the things I know about are really important, not just mirages.

ZENOBIA: So this noise isn't really important?

FATHER: Basically, no.

MOTHER: It's an image.

FATHER: A symbol.

MOTHER: A reference point.

FATHER: A warning. But one mustn't confuse the image, the signal, the symbol, the reference, and the warning with the thing itself. That would be an awful mistake.

MOTHER: A confusion.

FATHER: You keep out of this discussion. After all, this child is your daughter.

ZENOBIA: But if it isn't really important why do we leave?

FATHER: It's more prudent.

ZENOBIA: It's more prudent, even if it means leaving a six-room apartment where we were alone, and ending up in two rooms where. . . ! (*She looks at the schmürz.*)

FATHER: Prudence above all. (*He goes up to the schmürz, spits on it, and returns.*)

ZENOBIA: I had my own room, a phonograph and records, now I've got nothing and everything has to start off again from scratch.

FATHER: From scratch! You seem to forget this handsome antique sideboard.

MOTHER: You've really nothing to complain about. Think of the others.

ZENOBIA: What others?

MOTHER: There are others less fortunate than you.

FATHER: Than us. (*In a satisfied tone.*) Ha, yes. Two rooms, the way things are going . . .

MOTHER (*reciting*): Where they are going, no one can say,
But they knock on each door then go on their way.
(*She suddenly breaks off.*) No—that's not it. . . .

FATHER: That was fine to start with, why don't you go on?

MOTHER: Lassitude.

FATHER: Personally, I'm very pleased with this staircase.
(*He goes to it and slaps it with the flat of his hand.*)
It's oak.

MOTHER: It's beech made to look like oak.

FATHER: Beech, no. Pine, if you like, but not beech. That's
a wood far too . . . eh . . . um . . . beech, I'm talking
about.

MOTHER: Where's the kitchen?

FATHER (*pointing at a door*): It must be through there.

ZENOBIA (*speaking in a vague singsong voice*): Downstairs
I had my own room, painted blue like for a boy; my
little writing desk against the wall in the center, with
my movie star album in the right-hand drawer, my
school exercise books underneath, and my other books
along the shelf. Through the window I could see
the green trees, the sun always passed by, they were
years with twelve months of May, months of May
with thirty-one Sundays, Sundays which smelled of
fresh wax and English candy, and a lace bedspread
on my bed, it wasn't real lace but it was oh so pretty,
we used to dip it in cold tea so that it was just the
color of brown bread. And I went dancing every
Sunday night.

MOTHER: Darling, children your age shouldn't live on memories.

She starts tidying and shifting things. The FATHER *has opened all the doors, the wall cupboards, the sideboard doors, giving an occasional punch to the schmürz meanwhile.*

FATHER: This is the landing-door, so called because it leads on to the landing.

ZENOBIA: And what does it lead?

FATHER: Zenobia, please don't take everything so literally. You're making me dizzy.

ZENOBIA (*muttering*): Literally! (*She shrugs her shoulders.*)

FATHER: Zenobia, it's time you did your homework.

The FATHER *walks out on to the landing, and can be seen examining the door of the apartment opposite. He comes in again while* ZENOBIA *is wandering distractedly around the room.*

Our neighbor seems respectable and prosperous.

MOTHER: You saw him?

FATHER: No, I saw his name on the door.

MOTHER: Names don't make people. You've said that to me often enough yourself.

FATHER: He's an adviser.

MOTHER: That might be useful.

MUG *re-enters.*

MUG: What shall I make for lunch?

ZENOBIA: For lunch or for us?

MUG: What shall I cook?

MOTHER: We could eat leftovers.

ZENOBIA: Who's left over?

FATHER: What leftovers?

MUG: Veal, soup, radishes, semolina, turbot, carrots, or fish cakes. Or, if you like, eel, salami, stewed lamb, pig's head brawn, or mussels?

MOTHER: But what have we got in the cupboard?

MUG: Noodles.

FATHER: I don't want noodles. Still, after a night like that . . .

MOTHER: Make some noodles, since there's nothing else.

MUG: What's the point of making noodles when we already have some?

MOTHER: Well, cook some, then.

MUG: All right. (*She exits toward the kitchen.*)

FATHER: I wonder what kind of advice he gives?

MOTHER: Who? (*She goes and hits the schmürz.*)

FATHER (*dropping into an armchair and lighting his pipe*): The neighbor.

MOTHER: Ah, the adviser.

ZENOBIA: Mother, can I put on the radio?

MOTHER (*to* FATHER): Can she put on the radio?

FATHER: The radio . . . (*He scratches his head.*) Where is it? I wrapped it in the yellow checked bedspread. Did you take it?

MOTHER: No . . . I had the old black suitcase, the bag of linen, and the provisions.

FATHER: Well, I had the wicker basket, the toolbox, the planks . . . (*He calls:*) Mug! Mug!

She enters.

MOTHER: We can't find the radio. What were you carrying when we arrived?

MUG: The floor lamp, the pots and pans, the portrait of your cousin, the iron trunk, the bottle-rack, the shoe box, the vacuum cleaner, and my own things . . .

FATHER: And of course you forgot the yellow bedspread.

MUG: No one told me to take it.

She goes over to the schmürz and hits it. The MOTHER *shakes her head.*

FATHER: Ah well, we'll have to do without the radio.

MOTHER: Anyhow, we never listen to it.

ZENOBIA *exits.*

The child seems annoyed.

FATHER: Why?

MOTHER: I don't know.

A silence.

FATHER: I'm going to visit our neighbor.

MOTHER: Yes, go on, it'll give you something to do.

> *She takes up some sewing while the* FATHER *opens the door and leaves it open. He can be seen knocking at the door opposite. It opens. He goes in and the door closes again. Silence.* ZENOBIA *returns.*

ZENOBIA (*threateningly*): And what's going to happen now?

MOTHER (*sewing*): Your father's going to see to all that.

ZENOBIA: It's going to be just like before, only a little worse. We'll be a little worse off, we'll go through the same motions a little less briskly, do the same jobs a little less carefully. The nights will pass, the days will be like the nights, and then suddenly we'll hear the noise, we'll climb the stairs, we'll leave something behind by mistake . . . and we'll only have a single room . . . with someone already in it.

MOTHER (*fondly*): Now, now, dear, you're talking nonsense.

ZENOBIA: But what about me? What happens to me?

MOTHER: I've told you, your father is taking care of everything. There are all sorts of possible solutions.

ZENOBIA: At least you admit there's a problem?

MOTHER: Zenobia, you're irritating me. Children shouldn't pose problems to their parents except insofar as their parents recognize them as problems.

ZENOBIA: Recognize what? The children or the problems?

MOTHER: We have no problems, thank God. (*She gets up and stabs the schmürz savagely with her scissors.*) I can't imagine what can be troubling you.

> *The* FATHER *enters, accompanied by the* NEIGHBOR.

FATHER: Let me introduce my small family to you. Anna, my wife . . . Zenobia, my daughter.

NEIGHBOR: Madam! (*He bows.*)

FATHER: Mr. Garret . . .

ZENOBIA: We've known him for ages.

Silence.

He was already living across from us when I had my own room and my phonograph records.

FATHER (*clearing his throat*): Ahem . . . ah, well, there's no need for me to show you around our apartment, since your own is identical.

ZENOBIA: And then, when we went up one flight, he was still there living on our floor . . .

FATHER (*speaking loudly*): This sideboard, as you can see, is no less magnificent than your own. . . .

The NEIGHBOR *looks at the schmürz.*

NEIGHBOR (*in a low voice*): Yes, just like ours.

FATHER (*similar voice*): Indeed . . . personally, I find they all look alike . . .

The NEIGHBOR *gives the schmürz a kick.*

ZENOBIA: And then later, when we went up one flight more, he did the same.

NEIGHBOR: What a memory the girl has!

FATHER (*flattered*): Yes, what do you think of it?

NEIGHBOR: Ah yes, children are astonishing these days.

FATHER (*intrigued*): What do you mean exactly by that?

NEIGHBOR: Well, in the old days, you know, they were quite different.

MOTHER (*agreeing*): How right you are.

ZENOBIA: Different from *what* in the old days? You were children yourselves in the old days. So how can you make any comparison?

NEIGHBOR (*to the* FATHER): One can certainly see that your daughter's a brainy girl.

FATHER (*launching into an explanation*): Now, Zenobia, surely you can understand that a comparison can extend to a previous period of time?

ZENOBIA: But *who* compares, at that particular moment? You, with your idiotic mentality, are certainly not in a position to compare the child that you were once upon a time with the young girl that I am at this moment.

FATHER: Zenobia, you're going too far.

NEIGHBOR: Your daughter has nevertheless put her finger on something. The problem of the impartial observer.

ZENOBIA: There's no such person.

NEIGHBOR (*sitting down*): I would be curious to ascertain your point of view.

ZENOBIA: If he observes, he's not impartial; he already has a desire, that of observing. Otherwise, he observes distractedly. And is no longer a good observer.

FATHER: He may . . . eh . . . he may be impartial by constitution. (*He goes and strikes the schmürz and returns.*)

ZENOBIA: And who, may one ask, has constituted him?

NEIGHBOR: His education may have been such as to endow him with impartiality.

ZENOBIA: What education? The one his parents give him? (*She sniffs disgustedly.*) And who's to judge if he's received an impartial education? His parents? They are probably partial in every sense of the word, if in fact they really are his parents at all.

FATHER (*bursts out*): This is outrageous. Will you be quiet immediately?

ZENOBIA (*very calmly*): I am being quiet.

> *She is silent. Silence. The* NEIGHBOR *drums on his knees. The* MOTHER *goes over to hit the schmürz, which is sticking adhesive tape all over itself. She tears some off it and has difficulty in unsticking it from her own hands.*

NEIGHBOR: Your daughter is charming.

FATHER (*mollified*): There . . . at last we have it . . . that is exactly the remark with which you should have started. That makes things easier for me. To continue . . . (*in a man-of-the-world voice*) your own son, whom I glimpsed in the passage, seems to be quite a man!

ZENOBIA: Are you going to start all over again, trying to make me play with his son? I'm a little old for that sort of thing.

FATHER (*harshly*): Shut up! (*To the* NEIGHBOR:) He must be quite a handful, the brute, eh? Ha! ha!

NEIGHBOR: Well, he is approaching eighteen . . .

ZENOBIA: And how does he approach it? On foot? On horseback? Or on roller skates?

MOTHER (*to* NEIGHBOR): You should bring him over; it would be fun for the dear girl.

ZENOBIA: If Xavier wants to see me, he doesn't need his father to bring him.

Each time that ZENOBIA *speaks, no one listens to her.*

NEIGHBOR: Thank you very much for the kind invitation. Xavier will be delighted to have the opportunity of making friends with Zenobia.

FATHER (*to the* MOTHER): What should I say now, do you think?

MOTHER: Wait a moment . . . she's not as young as the last time. I think one should—

She whispers something in his ear. The NEIGHBOR *has got up and viciously twists one of the arms of the schmürz, then returns and sits down again.*

FATHER: You are right.

MOTHER: The whole affair depends on it.

FATHER (*to* NEIGHBOR): Exactly what do we propose in this matter?

NEIGHBOR: At their age it seems to me that . . .

MOTHER (urgently, to FATHER): Naturally, Léon. Love . . .

FATHER: Very well. (*He rises and announces:*) Profession of faith.

ZENOBIA: Oh, for goodness' sake . . . (*She gets up, crosses the room and exits into the kitchen.*)

MOTHER (*to* NEIGHBOR) : She's so well brought up, don't you think? So discreet!

NEIGHBOR: I find her charming. My son is a lucky dog!

FATHER: One minute! (*He starts off again.*) Profession of faith!

A pause.

I am not one of those tyrannical characters, of which nature and literature provide copious examples, such as disgrace world culture and the progress of genuine human civilization. (*He wipes his forehead.*)

MOTHER (*in a low voice*): Léon, that's the best opening sentence I've ever heard you speak.

The FATHER *gestures to her to be quiet and carries on. The* NEIGHBOR *is listening in a self-important posture; he picks up the ash tray and hurls it at the schmürz's head.*

FATHER: Furthermore, if it depended solely on myself, all false senses of security would long ago have been replaced by those truly gilt-edged securities: morality, progressive ideas, the advance of the physical sciences, street-lighting and the crushing of all the rotten remnants of an increasingly disintegrating demagogy, in the manner . . . eh . . . in the manner of those great builders of other ages who based their enterprises on a sense of duty and of public responsibility . . .

NEIGHBOR: Are you not perhaps losing the thread somewhat?

MOTHER (*to* NEIGHBOR): Yes . . . I have a feeling that he may not be going in quite the direction he intends.

FATHER (*in his natural voice*): Damn. I've the same impression. I'm afraid I'm being carried away by words.

MOTHER: If you remember, it's a question of your daughter and his son.

NEIGHBOR: Nothing should ever be a question of anything else. Youth should be at the center of all public preoccupations.

FATHER: I'll try to get back to the subject. (*In a declamatory voice.*) How beautiful it is to see the young buds blossoming all around one. (*He stops abruptly.*)

MOTHER: Go on, that sounded good . . .

FATHER: I'm running short of adjectives . . .

Enter MUG.

MUG: This kitchen is revolting, disgusting, horrible, dirty, lousy, sordid, nauseating, unmentionable, pustulant, rotting, peeling, malodorous, repulsive, et cetera. (*A pause, then furiously.*) And yet I'm going back into it. (*She exits.*)

MOTHER: Now, *there's* an example for you!

FATHER: Oh! It's easy enough to find disparaging epithets . . . But, come now, the buds, yes, yes . . . Develop the theme, my dear.

MOTHER: The young verdant buds.

FATHER: No . . . Verdant is clumsy. I wish to evoke the tender green of hazel catkins; or the pale hue of the lime blossom that takes on a hint of color and darkens delicately at the base of this fragile vegetable efflorescence to turn a pistachio-green; that subtle hue that makes one's heart become a lump in one's throat as one strolls in springtime along a country lane deep in shit.

MOTHER: Oh! Léon!

FATHER (*furiously*): Well, it's true, isn't it? Those swine always come and pull their pants down wherever it's prettiest. Why, I want to know, why? (*He is nearly screaming.*)

MOTHER: Calm down.

FATHER (*calming himself*): You're right. (*Declaiming.*) What a joy it will be for us to see those two young heads tenderly intertwined . . . eh . . . intertwined by the ears . . .

MOTHER: Léon! You're raving!

FATHER: Listen, I said "these two young heads intertwined" —they must be intertwined by something . . .

MOTHER: By their arms . . .

FATHER: Heads don't have arms.

NEIGHBOR: Nothing which is abstract has arms, dear madam. Agriculture, for instance.

MOTHER: And the Venus de Milo, is that abstract?

The FATHER, *inattentive and pensive, goes over to hit the schmürz and returns.*

FATHER (*smacks the table*) : We're drifting, we're drifting. (*To the* MOTHER:) Shall I ask now?

MOTHER: No, not so fast . . . and besides, it's for him to do that. It's the father of the young man who has to ask for the hand of a young girl.

ZENOBIA *re-enters.*

ZENOBIA: The kitchen is filthy. Are you all *still* making fools of yourselves?

MOTHER (*to* NEIGHBOR): She's *so* high-spirited, but I'm modern in outlook, and I believe young people today should be allowed to speak frankly.

The schmürz slumps to the ground, the FATHER *looks at it, goes into the kitchen, returns with a jug of water and empties it over the schmürz's head; the schmürz struggles to its feet again painfully, and the* FATHER *kicks it in the face. During this time, the* MOTHER *goes on speaking.*

Although I'm an advocate . . . or advocant . . . or advocess, that's it, although I'm an advocess of strictness with small children to teach them that everything in life isn't jam, I believe strongly that, once the cape of tender years has been safely rounded, one should let these little white ships sail on a bowline, with the wind on the quarter, on the tepid waters of existence.

ZENOBIA: A completely idiotic theory incidentally. (*She takes a good bite from her sandwich.*)

NEIGHBOR: She will get on splendidly with Xavier.

ZENOBIA, *worn out, sits down in a chair, takes off one shoe and scratches her foot. One can just hear vaguely the Noise outside. Immediately, the* FATHER, *the* MOTHER, *and the* NEIGHBOR *sit upright.* MUG *enters. The schmürz is the only one not frozen still.* ZENOBIA *stops scratching herself, terrified. The Noise ceases; everyone except the schmürz seems relieved.*

MOTHER: I have a feeling that we shan't have time to get used to this delightful apartment.

MUG: Well, do I stop work, then, or do I go on washing, scrubbing, beating, scouring, brushing, shining up, repairing, cleaning, scraping, sweeping, waxing, dusting and polishing?

MOTHER: Carry on, of course, carry on.

FATHER: We'll be here for some time. Speaking offhand, I'd say for at least . . . for at least a certain period.

NEIGHBOR: I have the same impression, but it would perhaps be wise for me to return to my own quarters to verify the supposition in my account book.

FATHER (*showing him to the door*): Must you go? (*He shoves him out.*) Good-by. (*He closes the door again.*) Wow! What a bore.

MOTHER: My! Yes. But, you know, I think the child is right. I seem to remember his face.

FATHER (*not listening*): Still, one is better off with a family around one.

He starts searching among the packages, and finds a dog whip. He takes off his jacket and begins to flog the schmürz with an incredible savagery.

MOTHER: It's the mole near his nose, in particular, that gives me the idea I've already seen him. But where and when?

FATHER (*in his normal voice*): Yes, his features do seem familiar.

MOTHER: Ordinary.

FATHER: Vulgar, even.

ZENOBIA (*dreaming*): When I had my room and my records, Xavier had the same room as I did on the other side of the courtyard, and we swapped records all the time. Like that, we each had twice as many. His father is as stupid as ever. (*She looks at her* FATHER *and screams out*:) But what are you doing to it? What are you doing to it? Leave it alone!

FATHER (*turning to her, his face completely expressionless*): Where's Mug with the noodles?

MOTHER (*face expressionless*): That's right. They should be ready.

ZENOBIA *rushes out into the kitchen, overwhelmed.*

FATHER (*continues flogging for a moment, then stops and calmly rubs his hands together, and cracks his knuckles*): Would you like me to unpack the black suitcase? We've got time before Mug sets the table.

MOTHER: That *would* be very useful, darling. I think the forks are at the bottom. And don't forget the partition will you?

FATHER: No, no. I'll fix it up as soon as the meal's over. (*He rubs his hands, looks around him.*) Well, speaking for myself, I'm feeling quite at home already. (*He gives her a kiss.*)

Enter MUG *with a steaming dish, and* ZENOBIA *with some bread and a jug of water. The* MOTHER *arranges the plates and silverware.*

ZENOBIA (*who has seen her parents kissing*): No, listen, really, you're getting too old . . .

MOTHER: One's never too old for that when one's in love.

ZENOBIA: In that case, it's me that's too old to watch it; it disgusts me. It really disgusts me.

The FATHER *and* MOTHER *have sat down and are settling themselves.*

FATHER: Love is never ridiculous.

ZENOBIA: Love, perhaps. (*She sits down.*) I'm not hungry.

MUG *starts to serve.*

MUG: It's getting cold.

The FATHER *serves.*

FATHER: Hm! . . . That smells good.

MUG: It smells of noodles.

MOTHER: They look very good. Leave the dish, Mug, my dear, we'll help ourselves.

MUG *gives her the dish and retires, giving the schmürz a wide berth. The* FATHER *eats without seeming to notice her absence. When she gets to the kitchen, he calls out, peremptorily:*

FATHER: Mug . . . haven't you forgotten something?

Resignedly, MUG *returns, takes the whip and begins to flog the schmürz.*

MOTHER: This is excellent!

ZENOBIA *drops her head to her chest and then puts her hands over her ears, her head and shoulders flat on the table, while the* MOTHER *and* FATHER *eat and while* MUG *goes on flogging. The curtain starts falling slowly.* MUG *stops and exits.*

FATHER: Splendid!

MOTHER: Very good!

FATHER: Succulent!

MOTHER: Delicious!

Curtain

ACT TWO

A different stage set. This new room is just below the attic, with a partially sloping ceiling, and is even drabber looking than the room in Act One. Exactly the same props, and the suitcases and bundles which were dragged up from the floor below at the beginning of the play. But there are fewer doors. This is more of a studio than a living room; there is a hot plate on one table, a washbasin on another, and so on. Upstage, a door opening on to the landing, as in the previous act. But there is just one other door now, leading to the only other room, in which the parents and MUG *sleep.* ZENOBIA *is lying down on a shabby couch. The schmürz, in an even more ghastly state than before, is bandaging itself with some filthy old rags, paying special attention to a bleeding wound on one of its legs, from which it occasionally flicks away the flies with a rag.*

When the curtain rises, ZENOBIA *is seen stretched out on the couch, and* MUG *is sitting on its edge, unraveling the wool from an old sweater and winding it into a ball.*

In a corner of the room is a staircase, as in the previous act, but narrower and more rickety.

ZENOBIA: What day is it?

MUG: Monday, Saturday, Tuesday, Thursday, Easter,

Christmas, Whitsunday, Wet Sunday, What Sunday, or no Sunday at all, probably.

ZENOBIA: Just as I thought. Time passes slowly.

MUG: There's no room.

ZENOBIA: Are there too many people, or what? What's stopping it from passing? Anyhow, where is it passing? Through the eye of a needle? In the street?

MUG: It went this way. It will go that way next time.

ZENOBIA: Give it a glass of water while they're out of the room.

MUG (*looking at her woodenly*): What?

ZENOBIA (*pointing her chin at the schmürz*): Give it a glass of water.

MUG (*blankly*): Give *what* a glass of water?

ZENOBIA (*silence—she shrugs her shoulders, and does not pursue the subject*): Give me a glass of water.

MUG *looks at her dubiously.*

I'm thirsty.

MUG: Are you sure you're thirsty?

ZENOBIA: No. I wanted to give it to *it*.

MUG: What are you talking about?

ZENOBIA *gives her a long glance, then looks away.*

ZENOBIA: Why am I lying down?

MUG: You are not well. You are in ill health. You are indisposed. You are showing preliminary symptoms of an upset system. Your state of health seems unsatisfactory.

ZENOBIA: I'm ill?

MUG: One can't really say that you are *ill*.

ZENOBIA: It's the stairs. We climbed them too quickly. (*She looks around.*) We can hardly sink much lower.

MUG: We've no kitchen any longer.

ZENOBIA: Just a bedroom, and this room. What's the proper name for a room like this?

MUG: It hasn't even got an improper name. But you could call it a poke-hole, a closet, a garret, a brothel, a wall cupboard, a shitting room, and a lot of other things besides, not to mention a rattrap, though there aren't any rats. At least, I hope not.

ZENOBIA: Why am I ill?

MUG: Well, I'm not feeling so brilliant myself. As for your father and mother, one can detect symptoms . . .

ZENOBIA: What kind?

MUG (*shrugs her shoulders*): Oh, symptoms of a disquieting kind.

ZENOBIA: Apart from their absolute idiocy, I've never detected anything at all in them.

MUG (*looks her straight in the eye*): Nothing?

ZENOBIA (*after a silence*): What are you going to use that wool for?

MUG: A sweater, a jumper, a garment, a pull-over, a jacket, a piece of crochet work, a jersey, a camisole.

ZENOBIA: A cardigan.

MUG: There's not enough wool for a cardigan. This is worn out at the elbows. So the next one will be sleeveless.

ZENOBIA: A chasuble.

MUG: Maybe I won't have time to finish it.

ZENOBIA: What is the noise, Mug?

MUG (*turning her face away*) : What noise?

ZENOBIA: The Noise . . .

MUG: There are a thousand different kinds of noises. If they are not just animal noises they are probably . . .

ZENOBIA (*interrupting her*): No . . . *the* Noise . . . every time we leave . . . every time we get up in the middle of the night and climb the staircase, behaving crazily, forgetting everything, hurting ourselves . . . Why can't we stay, once, just once? Why are we scared, like that? . . . It's so ludicrous . . .

MUG: We're not scared . . . We just climb the stairs, that's all.

ZENOBIA: But *if* we stayed where we were? If we had stayed?

MUG: Nobody stays.

ZENOBIA: And what's going on downstairs at this moment? We can't hear a thing . . . We never hear a thing . . . Why don't we listen to what's going on down there? Why don't we go down again?

MUG: You're feverish. Your temperature is rising. You're

becoming hotter and hotter. You're undergoing an increasing molecular excitement.

ZENOBIA: Well, I want to go downstairs again.

The schmürz has moved slightly, and begins dragging itself slowly toward the staircase.

MUG: Your father has blocked up the stairway . . .

ZENOBIA: I'll unnail the planks . . . I want to go down . . . I want to go and see who's living in our place . . . Yes, I want to go all the way down, as far as the room I used to have, when I had a phonograph and could listen to music.

She gets up, stumbling like someone weak with fever. MUG *supports her.*

MUG: Lie down again. Get back into bed. Stretch out. Rest. Calm down.

ZENOBIA *goes toward the staircase, sees the schmürz lying on the planks across the top of the stairs, crouched down like an animal, barring the way. She makes a despairing gesture and leans against the table.*

ZENOBIA: Give me a glass of water!

MUG *gets up, pours a glass of water from the jug standing in the washbasin, gives her the glass of water without looking at her and goes into the other room. As soon as she is alone,* ZENOBIA *takes the glass, approaches the schmürz, and holds the glass out toward it hesitatingly. With a quick movement, as if striking with a claw, it knocks the glass away and she shrinks back, frightened. She falls back on her couch and lies there sobbing, as* MUG *re-enters, picks up the glass,*

*wipes it and puts it back in its place, but avoids look-
ing at the schmürz. Then she goes up to* ZENOBIA *and
strokes her shoulder.*

MUG: Don't cry.

*ZENOBIA sits up, dries her eyes and blows her nose.
The door onto the landing opens, and the* MOTHER
enters followed by the FATHER. *They are both wearing
grave expressions.*

MOTHER: Poor man, it's really too bad.

FATHER: Yes—when you think of it, we're well off, com-
pared with him.

ZENOBIA is sitting on the bed; MUG *has left her and is
busying herself with various domestic tasks.*

ZENOBIA: How is Xavier?

MOTHER: Listen, sweetie, after all, you hardly knew the
young man.

FATHER: Yes, indeed. Since we've only been here for two
days, we should really think of Xavier as having just
been a good neighbor.

MOTHER: You can't take such an event to heart as if it had
been your brother, for instance.

FATHER: Your nephew.

MOTHER: Your cousin.

FATHER: Your son.

MOTHER: Or even your fiancé.

ZENOBIA (*coldly*) : Xavier is dead?

FATHER: Eh . . . unfortunately, it must be said that there is very little hope left.

MOTHER: He was buried yesterday, poor lamb.

ZENOBIA (*repeats, in a flat voice*): Xavier is dead.

MOTHER: His parents are simply stunned with grief.

FATHER: Ah, yes, they've certainly been hit very hard, poor people. We are really very lucky. (*He looks around, rubs his hands, goes over and strikes the schmürz, then returns.*)

MOTHER: We must admit that fate has hit them hard.

ZENOBIA: Oh, they'll make the best of a bad job. Everybody does. We do . . . (*she shrugs her shoulders*) . . . without even trying.

FATHER: We are very well off, Zenobia, I assure you—we are very well off.

ZENOBIA: What time is it?

MOTHER (*looks around, goes and hits the schmürz, returns*): I can't see the clock.

FATHER: I wrapped it up yesterday in the gray paper bag. Mug, weren't you carrying it?

MUG: No. (*She exits.*)

FATHER: Well . . . she's not very talkative today.

MOTHER (*to the* FATHER): So?

FATHER: We must have left it downstairs. (*He shrugs his shoulders.*) We don't really need it. The proof is that we've been here for two days without noticing that it was left behind.

MOTHER: It must be three-thirty or four . . .

ZENOBIA: If only I still had my phonograph, or even the radio . . .

MOTHER: What do you mean, the radio? You know we **never** had a radio, darling . . .

ZENOBIA: Before we were on the floor below . . . (*she points downward*) . . . we had a radio.

FATHER: I assure you that we had no radio when we were on the floor below. A clock, yes, that I grant you, there was a clock. But no radio.

ZENOBIA: I said "before we were on the floor below." If I'd meant "the floor below" I'd have said "before coming here."

MOTHER: Well, I pride myself on my good memory, and I don't remember any such thing as a radio. It's like the neighbor, poor man: your father tells me he's almost sure he met him before somewhere, and I do find his face familiar, myself, but I can't for the life of me recall our ever having been on friendly or any other terms with him. And yet, as I say, I've a very good memory, and just to give you an example, I can call to mind in a flash the proud, handsome profile of your father the day he led me to the altar.

FATHER (*to* MOTHER): We must take the child's mind off this business. (*Aloud.*) Of course, we hardly knew this Xavier, but I can quite see that through sheer human solidarity—I'll go further: through a spirit of across-the-hall loyalty—she is deeply moved by his departure and feels the need to clutch at any straw.

ZENOBIA (*looks at them*): It's really frightening how people of that age turn into driveling idiots.

The FATHER *goes over to the schmürz and gives it a good beating, finishing off with three kicks in the stomach.*

MOTHER: Is that all you feel about Xavier's disappearance?

ZENOBIA: I think he's damn lucky.

FATHER: Lucky? You funny child, you're not putting matters in perspective . . . Why, we've got a roof over our heads, something to eat, room to stretch ourselves in . . .

ZENOBIA: Less and less.

MOTHER: Less and less? Our neighbor is no better off than we are.

ZENOBIA: I don't give a goddamn about our neighbor. If he's satisfied with what he's got, that's his affair. The fact remains that he once had six rooms too.

FATHER: Six rooms! . . . Quite unnecessary.

The MOTHER *goes over and hits the schmürz.*

ZENOBIA: And how many floors are there still above us?

FATHER (*with absolutely genuine puzzlement*): I don't understand your question.

ZENOBIA: And if the Noise returns?

MOTHER: But what noise?

One can hear the Noise distantly, and all three stiffen immediately, except for the schmürz which continues to make slight movements.

ZENOBIA (*pale, with clenched fists*): If the Noise returns?

FATHER: We'll go upstairs. (*He goes over and examines the staircase.*)

ZENOBIA: What if there's nothing above us?

FATHER: This staircase must lead somewhere, you'll grant me that?

ZENOBIA (*patiently*): All right. But upstairs, there will only be *one* room.

FATHER: You can't possibly tell. It doesn't follow at all. You have no right to take it for granted that moving up one floor necessarily implies less space in the one above.

ZENOBIA: And if there's no staircase any longer, after we've moved up once again?

FATHER: If there's no staircase any longer, it will simply be because we won't need one any longer, and consequently you won't hear your precious noise any more.

ZENOBIA (*despondently*): If that's what you call reasoning . . .

FATHER: I really can't understand you, Zenobia. Lots of young girls would be only too happy to be in your shoes. (*He goes over and hits the schmürz.*)

MOTHER: You forget that she's a little feverish, the poor pet.

She goes up to ZENOBIA *and tries to fondle her, but* ZENOBIA *pulls away.*

ZENOBIA: What are you going to do now?

FATHER: What do you mean, "what are we going to do"? There's no question of doing anything. The wind is rising! . . . We must try to live!

MOTHER: She really is feverish, you know. (*To* ZENOBIA:) Go and lie down, sweetheart.

ZENOBIA *lets herself be led by the* MOTHER, *who makes her lie down and then goes and strikes the schmürz, and returns, while the* FATHER *turns the pages of a book and hums a tune.*

ZENOBIA: What did Xavier die of?

FATHER: I beg your pardon?

ZENOBIA: What did Xavier die of?

FATHER: Bah! Everything and nothing, you know perfectly well how people die when they're young.

ZENOBIA: No.

FATHER: Well, Xavier committed certain indiscretions, and his father made the mistake of not stopping him.

ZENOBIA: Did he go down the stairs?

FATHER (*annoyed*): I don't know.

ZENOBIA: Did he refuse to leave the floor below?

FATHER: Oh, I don't know, I tell you. The main thing is, he's dead.

ZENOBIA: He must have tried to go down; otherwise they wouldn't have buried him; if he'd stayed downstairs nobody would have dared to go and look for him.

FATHER: Bury him, bury him, well we assume they've buried him. If he was dead, it was the only thing to do, for goodness' sake. (*He goes over and strikes the schmürz.*)

The MOTHER *has left the room, returns now, and fusses around.*

ZENOBIA (*dreamily*): And what happened to John?

FATHER: John? (*He seems genuinely surprised.*)

MOTHER: Who are you talking about, Zenobia?

ZENOBIA (*dreamily*): When we lived in the apartment with four rooms and a balcony; right next to us, the neighbor's son used to come out on their half of the balcony and fly model airplanes. His name was John. He danced beautifully.

MOTHER: Zenobia, ducky, you're daydreaming.

ZENOBIA: I'm not dreaming.

MOTHER: Really, precious, your mother isn't as silly as all that, you know . . . (*To the* FATHER:) We must divert her; we've simply got to divert her. (*She goes over and strikes the schmürz.*)

FATHER (*reflectively*): But how? It is true that parents are entrusted with the task of shaping the character of their young children, insofar as it is in their power to do so, and giving them an education so refined that, when they emerge as fledglings from the family nest, their confrontation with the harsh realities of existence may be effected gently and naturally, without any hurt or anguish to their sensitive natures. But is it also the task of parents to divert their children, and does the shaping of a character permit the concept of diversion?

MOTHER: Educational diversion, yes. Xavier certainly

wasn't unique. We must help Zenobia prepare herself to find a new fiancé.

ZENOBIA: And, *if* I find this new fiancé, where are we supposed to live?

MOTHER: That's of no importance.

FATHER: The problem will resolve itself.

ZENOBIA (*sarcastically*): If it does, it will certainly be the only one. In any case, who's posing this problem?

MOTHER: I feel sure, after thinking about it, that example is the best guide. Our own example, under the circumstances.

FATHER: Our own example is, indeed, exemplary. (*To the* MOTHER:) Supposing I mimed our love affair?

MOTHER: Dearest, you are a marvelous mimic. But speak as well, don't limit yourself to mime. Why deprive yourself of a means of expression over which you have such complete mastery.

FATHER (*declaiming*): Reconstruction. (*He begins his recital.*) Let us picture a beautiful spring morning, the town in holiday mood, the bunting flapping in the breeze, and the roar of motor vehicles adding its note to the joyful clamor rising from this vast human ant heap. My heart was vibrating with electric impulses, and I was counting the hours—with the aid of a Chinese abacus bequeathed to me by my great-uncle: the one who took part in the looting of the Summer Palace in Peking. (*He stops short, and reflects.*) What happened to that abacus? (*To the* MOTHER:) Have you seen it lately?

MOTHER: Lord, no. But I'm sure we'll come across it when we start straightening up.

FATHER: No matter. The fact remains.

ZENOBIA: If all this happened in the past, the fact doesn't remain at all, of course. The fact that you remember it is a different matter altogether.

FATHER: Zenobia, I am trying to divert you; you are making me lose the thread.

ZENOBIA (*with indifference*): Oh, go on, go on.

She goes into the other room. The FATHER *continues his peroration.*

FATHER: In short, I counted the hours, and since mathematics was my strong subject this calculation presented no difficulties to me. No more did certain other calculations, such as that of the earth's circumference, or the number of grains of sand contained in a sand dune, for which one proceeds in the same way as when working out how many cannon balls there are in a stack, and so on. The caterers arrived in a never-ending stream at the happy bride's reception rooms, laden down with baskets of flowers and fruit . . . and dirty linen, since some people had mistaken the house for the laundry next door. But I can only repeat all this by hearsay, since she was at her home and I at mine. I was ready, resplendent; a healthy, upright air hovered around my well-shaven face, and, alone with my thoughts—in fact, really alone—I prepared myself for that fusion of identities, that change in civil status which has been called . . . hrrumph . . .

MOTHER (*reflectively*): Now who could have called it that?

FATHER: Come, come, on with the description! Take it up from where I left off.

MOTHER: Well, as for me, I was all blushes and shyness, though my parents were modern folk so that actually I knew quite well what to expect from this idle lout, and that once he was left alone with me he wouldn't be satisfied until he'd succeeded in shoving it in, meanwhile I was surrounded by my bridesmaids and chattering about this and that, all sorts of different subjects, because although a bride on her wedding day is thinking only of that one little thing, society forbids her to name the little thing before it's been tried out on her, that is except among primitive peoples, and really they're to be pitied, poor things!

The FATHER *returns from beating the schmürz.*

Léon, carry on, these reminiscences have exhausted me.

They continue to dance a sort of ballet, miming the whole marriage day.

FATHER: I was boiling over, my blood was bubbling, and when the blood starts bubbling, there's bound to be a clot.

The MOTHER *goes and strikes the schmürz.*

In fact, when my cousin Gautier—Jean-Louis Gautier, who was just completing his medical studies—came into the room, I said to him: "Don't you think a little bloodletting would do me good?" He roared with laughter. (*He roars with laughter.*) He laughed so hard that . . . I started laughing too. (*He goes up to the schmürz and rains blows on it.*) No, really, it was too funny for words. (*He stops and then says flatly:*) Ah, we certainly enjoyed ourselves that day.

MOTHER: I was twenty-two.

FATHER: I will pass on to the ceremony itself. (*He mimes.*) Do you take this ravishing little blonde to be your lawful wedded wife? You're not kidding, Mr. Mayor! What would *you* do in my place? As far as I'm concerned, said the mayor, I'm a queer. (*He slaps himself on the thigh.*) That was the best part of it. The mayor was queer.

MOTHER: Such a handsome man. What a shame.

FATHER: Then the priest got into the act: "Love, honor and obey," incense, choirboys, the collection, in short, the whole thing went off with a bang. There were five collections.

MOTHER: Are you sure?

FATHER: Well, I'm embroidering the story a bit, but I distinctly remember those five collections. The incident touched me deeply. Then lunch with my in-laws.

MUG *appears with a plate on which there are some slices of cold veal, and chicken legs.*

We stuffed . . .

MOTHER (*shocked*): Really!

FATHER: We stuffed ourselves with food.

He takes the plate from MUG *and begins to eat.* MUG *moves toward the door, steering clear of the schmürz. The* FATHER *snaps his fingers peremptorily, she returns and hits the schmürz.*

The champagne flowed in intoxicating waves.

MOTHER: The sparkling wine.

FATHER: It's true, your parents always were stingy.

ZENOBIA *enters, munching a sandwich.*

ZENOBIA: Haven't you finished your *Son et Lumière* yet?

FATHER: As for the sequel, I leave it to your imagination. Just we two alone, married that very morning, in the little room . . .

ZENOBIA (*interrupts*): Nine months later I was born.

MOTHER: And we went to live in Arromanches, where you'd been offered a good job.

FATHER: Horse knacker. Rather like being a sculptor, but working on living material.

MOTHER: And here we are. A radiant household . . .

Their ballet comes to an end; she goes toward the FATHER *and he toward her, in such a way that their paths converge just in front of the schmürz, on which they proceed to rain blows.*

. . . happy, never at odds despite all adversity.

They continue beating the schmürz.

ZENOBIA (*in an expressionless voice*): Didn't anything happen since then? (*She sits on the edge of the bed.*)

FATHER (*moving forward*): Since when?

ZENOBIA: Since Arromanches?

FATHER: We have left the village for the big city . . . And we are carrying on our life together, a devoted couple, for better and for worse, and even for the same, since the better and the worse tend to be exceptional, like peak hours.

ZENOBIA: As far as the electricity supply is concerned there's nothing exceptional about peak hours. They happen every day.

MOTHER: Zenobia, I really can't think from whom you've inherited your argumentative nature.

ZENOBIA: From you—probably by contrast.

MOTHER: I've gone through all the members of the family in my mind, and I still can't imagine how on earth you ever acquired such a frame of mind, or who gave it you.

FATHER (*to the* MOTHER): If you like, we can start a methodical study of the family. Everything methodical enchants me. We could even draw up a genealogical tree. You could help me.

ZENOBIA: You'd do better to let it grow of its own accord. Personally, I'd drop it.

MUG *enters and carries on the conversation.*

MUG: She wants nothing to do with it, she's steering clear of all this, she gives up, she's packing the game in, she's hedging her bets, she's washing her hands of the whole affair, she's getting out while the going's good —in fact, she disassociates herself from the entire enterprise.

FATHER (*annoyed*): May one ask, Mug, what business this is of yours?

MUG: Who's asking this idiotic question?

FATHER: I am.

MUG: Then don't say "one." Say "May I ask what business this is of yours," or "Mug, what's it got to do with you," or "In what respect does this problem concern you," or "What possible interest can this matter have for you." But be direct, and don't proceed by allusions. Do *I* ever alluse? (*She seizes some piece of furniture and starts dusting it vigorously.*)

FATHER: Oh, for Christ's sake!

Furious, he goes to pour himself a glass of water, while the MOTHER, *who has not listened to a word of all this, after picking out a large needle—a hatpin or something similar—from a sewing basket, goes over to the schmürz and sticks the needle into it.*

I don't pay you to argue.

MUG: I have services to sell, and I sell them. At the price you pay for them, you've got a good bargain. And apart from the commercial aspect of the relationship, there's nothing to stop the seller from arguing with the buyer, especially if the goods aren't counterfeit. (*She hurls her apron onto the floor with a violent gesture.*) In any case, I'm shutting up shop.

FATHER: What do you mean, you're shutting up shop?

MUG: I'm not selling my services any longer. You can go and buy elsewhere. Or rather, I can go and sell my services elsewhere.

ZENOBIA: Mug . . . are you really going?

MUG: Listen, your father's just too stupid for words. Where and when does he think he is? I'm the only one here who's sitting pretty . . .

FATHER (*in a superior and sarcastic tone of voice*): And would you care to explain in what respect you are "sitting pretty"?

MUG: Because I'm selling services which are much in demand by slackers, idlers, good-for-nothings, wastrels, shirkers, and other redundant members of society, and there's no shortage of such creatures. (*She puts on her straw hat, picks up a small case and exits by the door onto the landing.*)

FATHER (*outraged*): Well, really! She was actually trying to tell me off!

MUG *re-enters, puts down her case, and hugs* ZENOBIA.

MUG: Good-by, sweetie. Be very careful. (*She picks up her case again, and starts to exit.*)

FATHER (*in a peremptory tone*): Mug . . . you're forgetting something . . .

MUG *looks around her, glances briefly at the schmürz, and shakes her head firmly.*

MUG: No . . . I've forgotten nothing, as far as I can see. (*She exits and closes the door behind her.*)

FATHER (*rubbing his hands together*): Phew! Good riddance. That girl was getting more and more insolent. I'm glad she's gone. (*He goes up to the schmürz and starts beating it.*) Anyhow, this will save us money, and we've practically got an extra room.

ZENOBIA (*coldly*): I'm not sleeping in here by myself.

FATHER: Well. Well, all right . . . then you can sleep in the other room, with us . . .

ZENOBIA: I could sleep by myself in the other room . . .

FATHER (*laughs*): How you do go on! The young lady must have the finest room . . .

ZENOBIA: Why do people have children? So as to give them the worst room?

MOTHER: Zenobia, calm down . . . To begin with, one doesn't always have children on purpose . . .

ZENOBIA (*harshly*): People who don't know the facts of life should control themselves.

Silence.

FATHER: *Hmm* . . . (*To the* MOTHER:) She really *is* growing up, isn't she?

MOTHER: Can we still consider her as a child?

FATHER: She is certainly approaching maturity.

MOTHER: She is an adolescent, but with all the essential adult features.

FATHER: I can see no reason why she should not get married. (*He goes and hits the schmürz.*)

MOTHER: And if she were married, shouldn't she be expected to sacrifice herself for her old parents?

FATHER: Especially since we are *already* installed in the other room . . .

The MOTHER *walks toward the other room, and turns the doorknob, but the door refuses to open. Suddenly she becomes panic-stricken.*

MOTHER (*in a low, tense voice*): Léon!

FATHER (*surprised, turns around, rubbing his hands together*): What's the matter with you? You scared me.

MOTHER: Léon . . . The door won't open.

FATHER: Don't say that . . . my black suitcase and my camera are in there . . . (*He goes to the door and tries to open it.*) Mug must have locked it when she left . . .

Far away, the Noise can be heard, and all except the schmürz stiffen to attention.

ZENOBIA (*apathetically*): Mug never went near the door.

The FATHER *tries once more unsuccessfully to open the door.*

FATHER: It's not locked . . . The handle seems to be jammed . . . as if it were welded . . .

ZENOBIA (*imitating Mug*): Stuck . . . immobilized . . . riveted . . . unyielding . . . unmovable, and, so to speak, unturnable. (*She bursts out laughing, but stops very quickly.*)

FATHER (*goes over to the landing-door, tries to open it and succeeds; then, jovially*): Ah ha! I felt sure this one was still working . . . come now, there's no reason to panic . . . (*He passes in front of the schmürz and takes the opportunity of giving it a beating.*) Everything's fine! . . . we've still got quite a large room, and luckily the hot plate and the washbasin are both in here. (*He laughs.*) My goodness, we'd have felt hemmed in, in the other room. . . . (*To* ZENOBIA:) Which, I must say, was not a particularly pleasant room, I can assure you . . . You'll be far better off in here, with us.

ZENOBIA: Of course.

FATHER: Nevertheless, I feel it my duty to take various elementary precautions. (*He goes to the staircase, and tests its solidity.*) Hmm . . . It seems more rickety than it was yesterday, don't you think so, Anna?

MOTHER: I've not really paid much attention to the matter, but if you say so, dearest, it's bound to be true . . .

The FATHER *takes a run and practices dashing up the stairs, several times.*

No . . . it still seems to be working all right . . .

He comes down the stairs.

Let's get organized. Where's the child going to sleep?

ZENOBIA: Oh, I'll be all right on the floor. (*She sits down, puts one hand to her head, and sways slightly.*)

MOTHER: Zenobia, don't be silly, we're going to fix up a cozy little corner for you. (*To the* FATHER:) Léon, I've got an idea: Perhaps you could borrow Xavier's bed from the neighbors.

FATHER: That's an excellent suggestion . . . (*He rubs his hands together.*) Although of course, it's rather awkward for me to ask him, in view of his recent bereavement.

MOTHER: Xavier was very fond of our little girl. (*She notices that* ZENOBIA *appears to be unwell.*) What's the matter, sweetheart?

ZENOBIA: I've got a slight headache.

The MOTHER *goes up to her and takes her pulse, while the* FATHER *scratches his chin and looks around him.*

MOTHER: It's nothing, just a slight fever . . .

ZENOBIA: I'd like some oranges.

MOTHER: Listen, angel, be reasonable . . . you know quite well that we're saving them for your daddy, who needs them because of his health . . .

ZENOBIA: Yes . . . but I want them all the same . . .

MOTHER: Zenobia, try to picture the present situation. We only have a very few oranges and your father is an adult man, a grown man; your father is no longer just a promise, he is a complete, perfected individual, who has given proofs of . . . oh . . . well . . . proofs. On the other hand, you are . . . let's say a lottery ticket; one can certainly wager on you but there *is* a risk involved. Mind you, I'm personally convinced that you'll turn out very well, but I do feel that for the moment, as between the flower and the fruit, it is wise to choose the fruit.

ZENOBIA: Is daddy the fruit?

MOTHER: It's a comparison, and that's all, my dear, but it is relevant, you see. The flower must sacrifice itself to the fruit.

ZENOBIA: Ah!

The FATHER *emerges from his meditations.*

FATHER: The best thing would be for the child to go herself and ask the neighbor for Xavier's bed. He surely won't refuse her. Whereas I feel uncomfortable at the thought of approaching him myself . . . It would be undignified for me . . .

MOTHER: Of course she'll be glad to go; and, after all, the bed *is* for her. Will you try to do this, precious?

ZENOBIA (*in a dead voice*): Of course . . . It's perfectly normal . . . Let everyone grab for himself.

MOTHER: Now you'll have a nice bed to sleep in tonight . . .

ZENOBIA: That's the main thing . . . (*She gets up.*)

FATHER: In any case, what can we lose by asking our neighbor for this bed? Eh? If he agrees, he agrees, if he refuses . . .

ZENOBIA: He refuses.

FATHER: There you are . . . There's absolutely no danger involved.

ZENOBIA (*leaning against the table*): You've never been able to see danger; how can you discuss it?

FATHER: I am aware of it when it exists. What makes you think you are able to see it better than I?

ZENOBIA (*looking at the schmürz*): I've seen it for a long time.

FATHER: Surely you're not scared of our neighbor? (*He laughs and goes over to hit the schmürz.*)

ZENOBIA: No . . . I'm not scared . . . of our neighbor . . .

She goes over to the landing-door and opens it. She can be seen crossing the landing, knocking at the Neighbor's door, waiting.

FATHER (*shouting*): Knock again . . . he must be there . . .

The MOTHER *goes over to assault the schmürz. The* FATHER *sits down with a book.* ZENOBIA *knocks once more, tries to turn the knob of the Neighbor's door, then comes back across the landing and speaks through the open door of their own apartment.*

ZENOBIA: His door seems to be jammed. . . .

FATHER: No, no, my dear child, just ring his bell . . . Come now, surely you're big enough to do a little thing like that by yourself?

ZENOBIA *shrugs her shoulders. She crosses the landing again, and knocks on the Neighbor's door. The Noise can be heard: a faint and distant echo. She hesitates, and removes her finger from the button of the Neighbor's doorbell, which she has been pressing. Gently, then suddenly very quickly, the family's landing-door closes with a bang. During this moment,* ZENOBIA *can be seen springing forward so as to get in before the door closes, but she is too late. She can be heard knocking on the door which has slammed in her face.*

The Noise grows louder and louder. The FATHER *and* MOTHER *are frozen into immobility. The* MOTHER *is horror-stricken and incapable of movement. The* FATHER *has dropped his book. The Noise grows fainter again. The* MOTHER *goes over to the landing-door and tries to open it. Her arm drops to her side after this unsuccessful attempt. The schmürz appears to be highly amused by the proceedings. The* MOTHER *re-*

turns, sits on the edge of the bed, and begins to smooth the bedspread mechanically. Zenobia's knocking has ceased. There is complete silence.

FATHER: Calm yourself, my dear . . . Children always end up by leaving their parents. That's life. (*He goes over and strikes the schmürz.*)

Curtain

ACT THREE

*An even smaller room than those in the preceding acts.
An attic. A single practicable window, through which
one can glimpse a patch of bright blue sky: one gets the
impression that the window is high above the ground. A
door which is unopenable; the head of a staircase, from
which the* FATHER *will shortly emerge. The room is dark
and gloomy, and badly furnished. A rickety iron bed. A
table. A cracked mirror. There is a schmürz in the room,
though it is obscured by the shadows when the curtain
first rises. There is no staircase leading up to the floor
above. In fact, there is no floor above. The Noise can be
heard in all its monotonous and repellent vibrancy.*

*Gleams of light come from the head of the staircase, which
ends at the attic's floor level. Faint sounds are audible of
activity below. The Mother's voice can be distinguished,
giving vent to indistinct cries of distress, followed by the
Father's voice, also from the floor below, but becoming
clearer as he climbs the stairs, just as he did at the beginning of Act One.*

FATHER (*turning around as he calls out*): The yellow bag.
. . . For goodness' sake don't forget the yellow bag,
Anna, the meat grinder's in it . . .

*He appears, dragging various packages behind him
with all his strength, and pushing other packages*

61

along in front of him; he goes down a few steps again and repeats the performance.

Anna! Anna! Are you coming or not? Hurry up, for goodness' sake . . . Pass me the yellow bag. (*Irritably.*) No, no, there's nothing to be afraid of! . . . Pass me the yellow bag, I say, we've got plenty of time. . . . (*He emerges, pushing a bag in front of him, and then goes down the stairs again.*) Now the small suitcase.

An indistinct murmur from the MOTHER.

Yes it *is* there, I tell you, it's by the dressing table, I packed it myself. . . . (*He goes down the stairs again, grips the small suitcase and reappears.*) I think there's only the bundle of linen left to bring up.

THE MOTHER'S VOICE: I won't have time.

FATHER: For God's sake, of course you've got time. . . . Ah! what a lot of fuss for nothing!

He starts down the stairs again, when suddenly a bloodcurdling scream can be heard from the MOTHER.

Anna! Anna! What's going on? (*He beats a hasty retreat up the stairs.*) Yes, of course I'm here, my love . . . Make an effort . . . Come down and fetch you? Don't be childish, Anna, for goodness' sake; my arms are full of packages. . . .

A second scream, like a death rattle.

Anna! Don't play games like that on me just to scare me, please. You're too old for that sort of thing . . .

He retreats hastily, extracts tools and planks from the baggage, and starts blocking up the mouth of the staircase; then he puts his ear to the ground, and in an anxious voice which is perhaps curious rather than anxious, calls:

Anna! (*To himself.*) Surely . . . it can't be possible . . . she really isn't answering any longer?

He listens, the Noise suddenly stops; nothing can be heard now except a vague sound of movement on the floor below.

Anna . . . You can't just desert people like that, you know . . .

Light begins to come through the window and falls on a schmürz standing in a corner of the room. The FATHER, *hammer in hand and nails in his mouth, frantically finishes sealing the stairway opening while talking aloud in a staccato manner.*

After twenty years of marriage . . . to abandon a man like that . . . Women are really incredible . . . (*He lifts his head.*) Incredible. (*He nails down the last plank and straightens up.*) There . . . that should be all right like that . . . (*He gets up, looks around the room, is momentarily startled at the sight of the schmürz.*) Let's see . . . Hmm . . . It's quite nice here . . . (*He walks around the room, keeping close to the walls.*) The walls are sound. (*He looks up.*) No leaks in the roof. (*He looks at the walls, and then tries the door, which appears to be locked.*) No door; or as good as none . . . that's to say, it will serve no useful function any longer, just as I thought. (*He kicks the schmürz in passing.*) Which is perfectly logical, as anyone could recognize. And I'm not just anyone. Far from it. (*He suddenly stands still.*) Who am I? (*Declaiming.*) Recapitulation. Dupont, Léon, age 49, teeth in excellent condition, vaccination marks tastefully distributed over the various limbs, height five feet eleven inches, which no one can fail to agree is above average, physically fit and of sound mind. Intelligence must also be considered as above average. Field of action; one room, no less, spacious enough for a man . . . hmm . . . for a single man. A man alone. (*Silence.*) For a single man. (*He laughs lightly.*) Yes, indeed, for a single man. Alone. That's the point. (*After a pause.*) Question: what does a man alone in his cell do? (*He corrects himself.*) Cell? That's too strong a word . . . After all, it possesses a window quite large enough to permit the passage of a man of perfectly normal girth . . . (*he goes over to the window*) . . . and allow him to . . . (*he looks out and downward, turns around, comes back*) . . . break his neck on the street below after falling from a height of roughly a hundred feet. (*He returns to the window.*) There's a little balcony on which I could, if I feared a lack of other diversions, which is not the case, grow pots of flowers: geraniums, sweet peas, morning-glory, nasturtiums, convolvulus, honeysuckle, hollyhocks. (*He interrupts himself.*) This way of enumerating things reminds me of someone, for some obscure reason. Who? That's the whole problem. Moreover, when I say "grow," it's a manner of speaking; let us face facts: these vegetables would get along very well without any assistance. (*He returns to the center of the room.*) But I had asked myself a question. What does a man alone in his . . . retreat do. Hmm. Retreat. The word is not quite accurate. That's to say that it is accurate, of course, if one considers one of its commonest meanings: the hermit in his retreat, the monk goes into retreat . . . But there is also the suggestion of "retreat" in retreat—running away from the enemy. Can this ascent of mine be considered as a running away? A man . . . (*he goes over and strikes the schmürz*) . . . worthy of the name never runs away. Running may be all right for noses or taps. (*He pauses, does not laugh.*) No . . . that doesn't make me laugh. How funny. But it is worth noticing, incidentally, that one *beats* a retreat. And why? Because of the enemy. So that by beating a retreat, one is, of course, beating the enemy at the same time. Thus, by a remarkable turn of fortune, this cell . . . this retreat . . . symbolizes my victory over the enemy. What enemy? (*A pause.*) That is what we have to decide.

A longish silence, during which he paces up and down the room in every direction, stopping finally in front of the small suitcase. Then he reassumes his recitative tone of voice.

I have not reached manhood without having demonstrated, like any other freedom-loving individual, my attachment to that invisible yet palpable entity, that intangible yet oh how thrilling phenomenon which we all refer to as the fatherland, although it is known by other names in foreign languages. Aided by my modest virtues, I have even acquired universally recognizable distinctions in the service of my country, discreetly manifested by a few gold pips on the sleeve of my coarse serge field jacket.

He bends down, is about to open the suitcase, then straightens up and begins to interrogate himself.

What motive impels me, at this moment, to reassume my uniform of field marshal of the reserve? Am I then a mere animal, reacting by instinct? NO! (*He draws*

away from the suitcase.) At the base of each of my
actions there lies a reasoning reason, a reasonable reserve, and an active intelligence which might be considered almost cybernetic were it not for the fact that
it is controlled by a law higher than myself: disinter-
estedness. (*He scratches his chin*.) Unquestionably, the
Noise is the reason for my ascent. And why should I
put on my uniform when I hear a noise? Ah, if some
dispatch-rider had entered the room, covered in blood
and caked with mud, flourishing a black-edged message
fraught with some bitter significance, crying out "To
arms!" or "Turn out the guard!" and collapsing hero-
ically onto the floor, then indeed I would be amply
justified in such a case if I . . . (*He taps the suitcase
with his foot*.) But what, in fact, happened? I heard
a Noise. I climbed the stairs. (*He goes up to the
schmürz*.) The situation is exactly the same as it was
on the floors below, apart from a few practical details.
And I am completely indifferent to practical details.
So . . . (*He warms to his theme*.) So, since . . . (*he
hits the schmürz*) . . . since everything is exactly the
same, one must strike at the roots . . . It is the Noise
which is responsible for everything. (*He laughs mockingly*.) At one time I pretended not to hear it when
it began to echo. Yes . . . setting an example . . . in
front of the family. (*He breaks off*.) . . . My family?
So I had a family. (*He reflects*.) . . . Sometimes I feel
as if I'm remembering things that happened to somebody else. (*He laughs*.) Somebody else! Whereas in fact
I'm all alone . . . that's really priceless. To return to
this noise—I am convinced that it must be a signal.
(*He breaks off. Then, pensively*.) I always felt sure
that it was only the absence of real tranquillity that
prevented my discovering the origin and basic pattern

of things. (*In a tone of satisfaction.*) Is this not the proof? I have a feeling that I am on the brink of a tremendous discovery. (*A pause.*) A signal. (*A pause.*) An alarm signal, primarily. My alarm signal. At least, as far as *I'm* concerned. Who is responsible for sounding the signal? (*A pause.*) Suppose the problem were resolved. I get the hell out. (*He corrects himself.*) No . . . I climb up one floor. Good. Why? Because I hear the signal. It is evident that the signal is therefore directed *against* the fact that I remain. Who, then, can be so annoyed by my remaining? (*He goes up to the schmürz and beats it.*) I ask myself, and I shall always ask myself. But that's how the world is made. This signal is directed *against* me. Therefore it is aggressive. It is a signal for attack. (*He returns to the suitcase.*) I am flabbergasted that anyone should desire to attack a man like myself. But one thing is certain. Attack entails defense. And defense entails . . . (*He bends over and opens the suitcase, taking out his uniform, which he displays.*) Fortunately, as far as defense is concerned, I am equipped and ready. (*He smooths out the uniform.*) Field marshal of the reserve . . . That may not be very much . . . but it will make them think twice before they try anything. (*He begins to change, taking off his clothes and putting on his uniform.*) So I am now clear about my situation. I am attacked. I defend myself. Or at least, I am preparing to defend myself. (*He looks around.*) Because of the absence of exits in this room, I am inclined to believe, as I have already said, that these attacks can no longer have any possible purpose. If they had wanted me to leave here they would, as I have already noted, have provided me with the means. (*A pause. He adjusts his uniform.*) My sword . . . (*He goes to another piece of baggage, takes his sword from it, and straps it on.*) I shall put on my cocked hat in due course, and if the occasion arises. (*A pause.*) I remember . . . (*A pause, then, coldly.*) No, I do not remember. A man of my age does not live in the past. I am in the process of building the future.

He approaches the schmürz silently and slowly, then suddenly hurls himself on it, throws it to the floor and begins to strangle it, keeping his grip while he continues to speak in a perfectly natural voice.

I think that what would look prettiest in the window would be sweet peas. And I'm so very fond of their scent.

He rises. The schmürz lies inert, but during the next few minutes begins to move again, and is finally up- right once more.

Sweet peas, which I shall harvest in due course, when the time is ripe, should the occasion arise; that is to say, generally speaking, when they are in flower. For I love flowers. (*He looks at himself.*) A warrior who loves flowers: that may seem preposterous, and yet I do love flowers. (*He winks.*) Does that imply that I am *not* a warrior? (*A pause. He draws himself up and announces:*) Confession. In reality—and what better moment to pounce upon reality, like a sparrow hawk upon its prey, than that in which man, isolated owing to the force of circumstances, finds himself face to face with his naked soul, just as an honest nudist does not hesitate to take stock of his neighbor's organs in order to see if they might, perchance, be bigger than his own—which is doubtless without significance, but the habit of making external appearances the basis of judgment is as deeply embedded in the human heart as the hermit crab in its shell. In reality, I say, despite this uniform, I represent in my own person a national characteristic by being fundamentally antimilitaristic. (*A pause.*) One may well lose oneself frequently in conjecture as to the reasons which make the hearts of an entire people beat faster with pleasure and desire at the very thought of a uniform. (*He laughs mockingly.*) Ha! The facts are quite simple really. The soldier's justification for existence is war. War's justification for existence is the enemy. An enemy dressed as a soldier is an enemy twice over in the eyes of an antimilitarist. For an antimilitarist is by no means devoid of national pride and seeks, therefore, to bring about the downfall of his nation's enemy. But what better way, if this enemy is dressed as a soldier, than to set up another soldier against him? It follows from these considerations that every antimilitarist has the duty to enter the army; in doing this, he accomplishes three feats: first, he irritates the enemy soldier; in addition, on his own territory, he is an object of displeasure to his fellow soldiers in other branches of the services, since a uniform has the particular virtue that people wearing different uniforms loathe each other on sight; but, apart from these factors, he also transforms himself into an element of an army which he detests and which will consequently be a bad army. For an antimilitaristic army carries its own cancer within itself and would be incapable of facing up to a true army composed of civil patriots. (*He scratches his chin.*) Can my enemy be considered civil? (*A pause. Then, in a different tone of voice.*) It is a mistake to devote to pure speculation time that could more profitably be occupied in examining realities which are tangible, audible, and, in one word, accessible to our organs of perception. For there are moments when I wonder if I am not simply playing with words. (*A pause. He looks out of the window.*) And supposing words were made for just that purpose? (*A pause, then he announces:*) Return to reality. (*He changes his tone of voice.*) This return to reality—interrupting a confession which started out most promisingly, I must say—seems essential nevertheless. It transpires, indeed, that I have ideas about practically everything; one only has to consider what I have discovered about a uniform—and a commonplace uniform of a field marshal of the reserve, at that!—to be convinced of that fact. I could have expressed my opinion on most major problems of humanity, which is more than most people are capable of doing . . . But is this not a delusion? For do not the major problems of humanity pose themselves only when man is living in society? (*A pause.*) Whereas I am alone. As I have already said.

He turns around and sees the schmürz, which has picked itself up and altered its position, being nearer the window now. He gives a sudden start, and one has the impression that he understands for the first time that he is confronted by something more than an object. He speaks as if in defense of himself.

I always had the impression that I was alone, in any case. (*A pause.*) I require evidence . . . a clear proof of any change, before I can persuade myself to revise this overwhelming impression. Have I been wrong or right to recapitulate before itemizing . . . to allow synthesis to precede analysis? (*He touches his eyes.*)

I see. (*He touches his ears.*) I hear . . . (*He breaks off, and announces:*) Inventory.

From this moment onward, he begins scrupulously avoiding the schmürz, while the schmürz, on the contrary, begins following him with its eyes with an increasingly steady attention.

There seems no reason why the world should extend very far beyond the walls which surround me; what is quite certain is that I am its center. (*Self-questioningly.*) Should I make a list of my internal organs? Perhaps that would be carrying analysis too far . . . (*He reflects.*) . . . and I only know my interior rather vaguely, by hearsay. It is quite possible that my heart causes my blood to circulate, but if it turned out that the movement of my blood was the real cause of my heartbeats . . . (*He interrupts himself.*) No, only the external organs. (*He goes up to the cracked mirror.*) With the aid of this apparatus I shall make faster progress. (*He looks at himself in the mirror and resumes his recitative tone.*) I have always asked myself what is the underlying motive which persuades a man to try and *direct* his physical appearance, especially by growing a beard. (*He strokes his beard.*) Therefore, in my anxiety to find an answer to this question, I grew a beard. And I am now in a position to reveal that as far as motive is concerned, there isn't any. I grew my beard to see *why* people grew beards. And all I found was a beard. The beard is the reason for the beard. (*He alters his tone of voice.*) Good beginning. No, my capabilities have certainly not been adversely affected by the altitude. (*He leans forward, annoyed, his hand to his forehead.*) I can't help feeling that there were once several of us here . . . and that the weather was cooler. (*He unstraps his uniform belt, and from this point starts removing the uniform gradually.*) This attic depresses me. (*Changing his tone of voice.*) When there were several of us, I retained the absolute majority. Now that there are no longer several of us, I feel my majority slipping away. Paradox, without a doubt, paradox . . . (*Changing his tone of voice again, as he fumbles in one of his suitcases.*) I used to have a revolver in addition to my sword . . . (*He has taken off his shoulder-belt and sword.*) . . . and I would prefer my revolver. (*He finds the revolver, and checks it over.*) It's a light, easily maneuverable weapon, which should provide just the support I need to reconquer my lost territories . . .

He grips the revolver and aims it at various targets; finally, he aims it at the schmürz, which is motionless but continues to follow his movements with its eyes. After a while he lowers the revolver.

I was discussing my beard. It is living, since it grows, and if I cut it it doesn't cry out. Neither does a plant. My beard is a plant. (*He goes up to the window.*) Nasturtiums, perhaps, instead of sweet peas? I could put them in salads . . . (*Reverting to his previous theme.*) A harmonious combination of flesh, bone, and pilosity, which brings together in the human male the animal, mineral, and vegetable kingdoms. (*Reflectively.*) One could say the same of any hairy animal. (*More confidently.*) Except that man is the only animal who is not an animal.

Suddenly he lifts his revolver and fires at the schmürz,

which does not flinch and seems unaffected by the shot.
A pause. He continues, in a rather tremulous voice.

As far as I can remember, this revolver was loaded
with blanks, otherwise I obviously wouldn't be so
crazy as to shoot at the walls of my room, at the risk
of injuring somebody.

From this point, he starts walking around the schmürz,
as though around a snake that is exercising an increas-
ingly hypnotic fascination.

People who allow themselves to be drawn into such
inconsiderate acts do not deserve to be attributed the
title of thinking reeds . . . "It moves for all that." (*He*
fires at the window, and a pane of glass shatters ex-
plosively.) Loaded with blanks. (*He looks at the re-*
volver and throws it away.) As far as I'm concerned,
this character can go to hell. One needs time to draw
up an inventory, and I haven't the time. I had it not
so long ago, on my mantelpiece, in a box. (*He kneels*
down, puts his ear to the ground and listens.) They
must have forgotten to wind it up. (*He has taken off*
his uniform, and is now in long underwear.) I no
longer have the time. I never had it. (*Silence.*) Life is
a scandal. (*He looks down at his legs, then scratches*
his chin.) I must get dressed.

He begins to rummage around in his bags and parcels,
and finally extracts some items of formal dress, includ-
ing a pair of gray striped trousers and a black jacket.

This suit reminds me of something. Some ceremony.
(*He shakes his head.*) No . . . These objects will be of
no use to me. (*He drops the jacket and puts on again*

the clothes he was wearing originally.) Ah, I feel more comfortable like this, there's no question about it. (*He notices a slight movement by the schmürz, and retreats. A long silence.*) Is it possible for the feeling of loneliness to develop in an adult individual except as a result of contact with his fellow creatures? No. If such is the case, this feeling of loneliness which I have always experienced was doubtless derived from one or more of the hypothetical personages by whom I was—perhaps—surrounded. I venture this opinion in order to assist the process of ratiocination that I am in the throes of formulating . . .

During the next few minutes, he extracts various objects from his baggage and pushes them near to the schmürz, as if placing offerings on an altar.

. . . at this moment. If I felt alone, it was exactly because I was not alone. It follows, therefore, that if I continue to feel alone . . .

He breaks off suddenly, goes up to the door, tries to turn the handle, then hammers at the door in a frenzy of rage and despair.

It's not true . . . I *am* alone . . . and I've *always* done my duty . . . more than my duty. (*A pause.*) We are racing toward the future at full speed, going so fast that we cannot glimpse the present, and the dust raised by our pounding feet hides the past from us. Whence the well-known expression . . . eh . . . whence the hundreds of well-known expressions which I could mention . . .

He is almost out of breath, gasping and breathing

*heavily. Then, after a pause, he assumes a very differ-
ent tone of voice—dead and broken.*

I am not alone, here.

*A very long pause, during which he searches for some-
thing which he does not find, without ever taking his
eyes off the schmürz. The Noise becomes gradually
audible, first very far away, then coming very, very
slowly nearer.*

Closing one's eyes to the evidence is a method which
has never been effective . . . For a blind man, well
and good, but . . . (*He interrupts himself.*) I can't hear
a thing. (*Louder.*) I can't hear a thing.

*Digging into the yellow bag, he extracts the meat
grinder, grips it, and starts turning the handle wearily.*

In those days there was at least the hope and promise
of a future generation which would wash the dirty
linen of its elders in a meat grinder. (*He shouts
out, while the Noise reaches a crescendo.*) I can't hear
a thing! (*He hurls away the meat grinder, and looks
at his hands.*) These hands are spotless. (*He looks
toward the window.*) The idea of nasturtiums wasn't
at all bad, but I feel that honeysuckle might be re-
warding on a wholly different plane . . . a higher plane
. . . It is not edible . . . I shall control my appetites.
(*He screams.*) I swear it! I shall control my appetites!
(*He shrugs his shoulders.*) So that I can get to know
them better and gratify them better. (*He throws himself onto his knees and screams.*) I can't hear a thing! I
can't hear a thing!

The Noise stops suddenly. The schmürz collapses,

visibly dead, alongside the wall where it had been standing. Sounds of knocking can be heard at the door. The FATHER *gets up from his knees.*

Accounts? I have no accounts to settle . . . I've always been alone.

The knocking becomes more urgent. He goes nearer to the window. The light begins to fade slowly.

Honeysuckle is not really as nice as convolvulus . . . Convolvulus is fresh and natural.

The knocking is louder and more insistent. He dashes up to the window, and gets one foot up onto the window ledge.

I've always been alone . . . I can't distinguish anything through the dust of the past . . . (*he totters, his foot slips, and he falls back, still hanging onto the window ledge*) . . . it covers people like dust-sheets . . . Furniture . . . They were all furniture . . . just furniture.

The knocking has stopped, the Noise suddenly recommences very close at hand. He gropes, trying to find some support for his foot.

I didn't know . . . Forgive me . . . (*He slips and falls to the floor, screaming.**) I didn't know . . .

The Noise invades the room, and darkness descends.

And perhaps the door opens, and perhaps schmürzes enter, vague outlines in the dark . . .

Curtain

* *Translator's Note*

It is fair to make clear here that the French has only *"Il glisse et tombe en hurlant,"* leaving it uncertain whether the Father falls out of the window or back into the room. In conversation with the author, I asked him about this ambiguity and he indicated that he envisaged the Father falling back onto the floor, which is why I have permitted myself to add the words "to the floor." However, the Royal Shakespeare Company production in London preferred to have the Father fall, screaming, *out* of the window, so that the stage is empty as the schmürzes "perhaps" invade the room as the curtain drops. It seems perfectly legitimate for the reader to choose this alternative interpretation of the final action if he wishes.

The schmürz
Production by Royal Shakespeare Company, London
Photo © by Morris Newcombe

Father, Mother, Zenobia, Mug
From the Brussels production. Photo © by Cayet

Zenobia, Mother, Mug, Father
London production. Photo © by Morris Newcombe

The schmürz
Théâtre Nationale Populaire production, Paris. Photo by Agnès Varda

Set for Act I
Malmö Stadsteater production, Sweden
Photo by Alice Stridh

Zenobia and Mug
Malmö production
Photo by Alice Stridh

Zenobia and Mug
London production
Photo © by Morris Newcombe

Zenobia and Mug
Brussels production
Photo © by Cayet

Mother, Zenobia, Mug, Father
London production
Photo © by Morris Newcombe

Mug, Zenobia, the schmürz
Paris production. Photo by Agnès Varda

The schmürz, Mother, Zenobia
Brussels production. Photo © by Cayet

Zenobia, Father, Mother, Mug, the schmürz
London production. Photo © by Morris Newcombe

Father, Zenobia, Mother, the schmürz, Mug
Paris production. Photo by Agnès Varda

Zenobia, Father, Mother, the schmürz
London production
Photo © by Morris Newcombe

Mother, the schmürz, Father
London production
Photo © by Morris Newcombe

Father and the schmürz
Paris production
Photo by Agnès Varda

Father
Paris production
Photo by Agnès Varda

Father, Mother, Zenobia, the schmürz
Schiller-Theater production, Berlin
Photo © by Heinz Köster

Father and the schmürz
London production. Photo © by Morris Newcombe

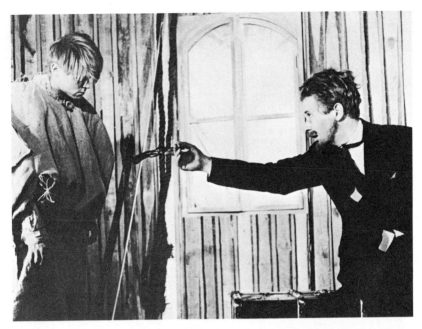

The schmürz and Father
Lilla Teatern production, Helsinki. Photo by Beata Bergström

The schmürz and Father
Ateliertheater production, Vienna. Photo © by Gretl Geiger

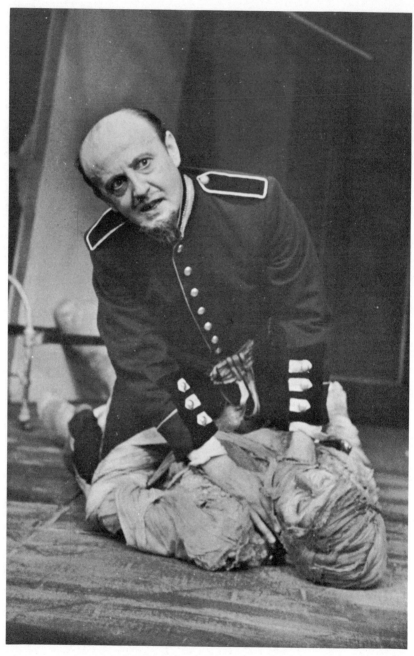

Father and the schmürz
London production. Photo © by Morris Newcombe

Father and the schmürz
Vienna production. Photo © by Gretl Geiger

The schmürz
Berlin production
Photo by Alice Stridh